BENJAMIN FRANKLIN

The Way to Wealth

Advertiſement.

This famous SPEECH moſt certainly does hit
The happy Point where Wiſdom joins with Wit.

AT the firſt Appearance of this humorous and inſtructive Production, ſeveral Gentlemen of approved *Taſte* were ſtruck with the Deſign and Beauty of it, and therefore deſired to know the *Parent's* Name.---Father *Abraham's* Speech is the comely *Off-ſpring* of that *Frank lyn-cean* GENIUS who is the Author of a Pamphlet intitled *The Intereſt of* Great Britain *conſidered*; and of the following Quotations from the Additions to ſaid Pamphlet, *viz.*

" The Legiſlator that makes effectual Laws for promoting of Trade, increaſing Employment, improving Land by more or better Tillage, providing more Food by Fiſheries, ſecuring Property, &c. and the Man that invents new Trades, Arts, or Manufactures, or new Improvements in Huſbandry, may be properly called FATHERS *of their Nation*, as they are the Cauſe of the Generation of Multitudes, by the Encouragement they afford to Marriage."

" The greater the common faſhionable Expence of any Rank of People, the more cautious they are of Marriage : Therefore Luxury ſhould never be ſuffered to become common."

" The great Increaſe of Offspring in particular Families, is not always owing to greater Fecundity of Nature, but ſometimes to Examples of Induſtry in the Heads, and induſtrious Education ; by which the Children are enabled to provide better for themſelves ; and their marrying early is encouraged from the Proſpect of good Subſiſtence."

" If there be a Sect therefore, in our Nation, that regard Frugality and Induſtry as religious Duties, and educate their Children therein, more than others commonly do ; ſuch Sect muſt conſequently increaſe more by natural Generation, than any other Sect in *Britain.*"

BENJAMIN FRANKLIN

Advice, Hints, and Tips on Business, Money, and Finance

ROWMAN & LITTLEFIELD
Lanham • Boulder • New York • London

Published by Rowman & Littlefield
A wholly owned subsidiary of The Rowman & Littlefield
Publishing Group, Inc.
4501 Forbes Boulevard, Suite 200, Lanham, Maryland 20706
www.rowman.com

16 Carlisle Street, London W1D 3BT, United Kingdom

Distributed by National Book Network

First Rowman & Littlefield edition published in 2014.

British Library Cataloguing in Publication Information Available

Library of Congress Cataloging-in-Publication Data Available

ISBN: 978-1-4422-2229-8 (cloth : alk. paper) — ISBN: 978-1-
4422-2230-4 (electronic)

♾™ The paper used in this publication meets the minimum
requirements of American National Standard for Information
Sciences—Permanence of Paper for Printed Library Materials,
ANSI/NISO Z39.48-1992.

Printed in the United States of America

Father *Abraham* in his STUDY.

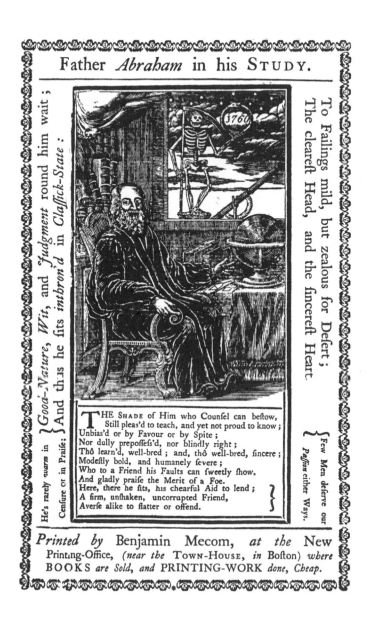

He's rarely warm in { Good-Nature, Wit, and Judgment round him wait ;
Cenſure or in Praiſe: { And thus he ſits inthron'd in Claſſick-State :

To Failings mild, but zealous for Deſert ;
The cleareſt Head, and the ſincereſt Heart.
{ Few Men deſerve our
Paſſion either Ways.

THE SHADE of Him who Counſel can beſtow,
  Still pleas'd to teach, and yet not proud to know ;
Unbias'd or by Favour or by Spite ;
Nor dully prepoſſeſs'd, nor blindly right ;
Thô learn'd, well-bred ; and, thô well-bred, ſincere ;
Modeſtly bold, and humanely ſevere ;
Who to a Friend his Faults can ſweetly ſhow,
And gladly praiſe the Merit of a Foe.
Here, there he ſits, his chearful Aid to lend ;
A firm, unſhaken, uncorrupted Friend,
Averſe alike to flatter or offend.

Printed by Benjamin Mecom, *at the* New
Printing-Office, *(near the* Town-House, *in* Boſton) *where*
BOOKS *are Sold, and* PRINTING-WORK *done, Cheap.*

FATHER
Abraham's
SPEECH

To a great Number of People,
at a Vendue of Merchant-
Goods;

Introduced to THE PUBLICK

By POOR *RICHARD*,

(A famous PENNSYLVANIAN Conjurer and
Almanack-Maker)

In Answer to the following Questions.

Pray, Father *Abraham*, what
think you of the Times? Won't
these heavy Taxes quite ruin the
Country? How shall we be ever
able to pay them? What would
you advise us to?

Printed and Sold by Benjamin Mecom, *at the* New
Printing-Office, *near the* Town-House, *in* BOSTON.

Father *Abraham*'s Speech, introduced by *Poor Richard*, viz.

CourTEOUS READER,

I Have heard that Nothing gives an Author so great Pleasure, as to find his Works respectfully quoted by other learned Authors. This Pleasure I have seldom enjoyed; for though I have been, if I may say it without Vanity, an *eminent Author* of Almanacks annually now a full Quarter of a Century, my Brother-Authors in the same Way, for what Reason I know not, have ever been very sparing in their Applauses; and no other Author has taken the least Notice of me, so that did not my Writings produce me some solid *Pudding*, the great Deficiency of *Praise* would have quite discouraged me.

I concluded at length, that the People were the best Judges of my Merit; for they buy my Works; and besides, in my Rambles, where I am not personally known, I have frequently heard one or other of my Adages repeated, with *as Poor Richard says*, at the End on't. This gave me some Satisfaction, as it shewed not only that my Instructions were regarded, but discovered likewise some Respect for my Authority; and I own that, to encourage the Practice of remembering and repeating those wise Sentences, I have sometimes *quoted myself*, with great Gravity.

COURTEOUS READER,

I Have heard that Nothing gives an author so great Pleasure, as to find his Works respectfully quoted by other learned Authors. This Pleasure I have seldom enjoyed; for though I have been, if I may say it without Vanity, an *eminent Author* of Almanacks annually now a full Quarter of a Century, my Brother-Authors in the same Way, for what Reason I know not, have ever been very sparing in their Applauses; and no other Author has taken the least Notice of me, so that did not my Writings produce me some solid *Pudding*, the great Deficiency of *Praise* would have quite discouraged me.

I concluded at length, that the People were the best Judges of my Merit; for they buy my Works; and besides, in my Rambles, where I am not personally known, I have frequently heard one or other of my Adages repeated, with *as Poor Richard says*, at the End of it. This gave me some Satisfaction, as it showed not only that my Instructions were regarded, but discovered likewise some Respect for my Authority; and I own that, to encourage the practice of remembering and repeating those wise Sentences, I have sometimes *quoted myself,* with great Gravity.

Father *Abraham*'s Speech.

Judge then how much I muft have been gratified by an Incident I am going to relate to you. I ftopt my Horfe lately where a great Number of People were collected at a Vendue of Merchant Goods. The Hour of Sale not being come, they were converfing on the Badnefs of the Times, and one of the Company call'd to a plain clean old Man, with white Locks, *Pray, Father* Abraham, *what think you of the Times? Won't thefe heavy Taxes quite ruin the Country? How fhall we be ever able to pay them? What would you advife us to?* --- Father *Abraham* ftood up and reply'd, If you'd have my Advice, I'll give it you in fhort, for *A Word to the Wife is enough*, and *Many Words won't fill a Bufhel*, as *Poor Richard* fays. They joined in defiring him to fpeak his Mind, and gathering round him, he proceeded as follows.

" *Friends and Neighbours,*

THE Taxes are indeed very heavy, and if thofe laid on by the Goverment were the only Ones we had to pay, we might more eafily difcharge them ; but we have many others, and much more grievous to fome of us. We are taxed twice as much by our *Idlenefs*, three times as much by our *Pride*, and four times as much by our *Folly*, and from thefe Taxes the Commiffioners cannot eafe or deliver us by allowing an Abatement. However, let us hearken to good Advice, and fomething may be done for us. *God helps them that help themfelves*, as *Poor Richard* fays, in his Almanack of 1733.

Judge then how much I must have been gratified by an Incident I am going to relate to you. I stopped my Horse lately where a great Number of People were collected at a Vendue of Merchant Goods. The Hour of Sale not being come, they were conversing on the Badness of the Times, and one of the Company called to a plain clean old Man, with white Locks, *Pray, Father* Abraham, *what think you of the Times? Won't these heavy Taxes quite ruin the Country? How shall we be ever able to pay them? What would you advise us to do?* Father *Abraham* stood up and replied, If you'd have my Advice, I'll give it you in short, for *A Word to the Wise is enough*, and *Many Words won't fill a Bushel*, as *Poor Richard* says. They joined in desiring him to speak his Mind, and gathering round him, he proceeded as follows.

"*Friends and Neighbors,*

THE Taxes are indeed very heavy, and if those laid on by the Government were the only Ones we had to pay, we might more easily discharge them; but we have many others, and much more grievous to some of us. We are taxed twice as much by our *Idleness*, three times as much by our *Pride*, and four times as much by our *Folly*, and from these Taxes the Commissioners cannot ease or deliver us by allowing an Abatement. However let us hearken to good Advice, and something may be done for us. *God helps them that help themselves*, as *Poor Richard* says, in his Almanack of 1733.

Father *Abraham*'s Speech.

It would be thought a hard Goverment that ſhould tax its People one tenth Part of their *Time*, to be employed in its Service. But *Idleneſs* taxes many of us much more, if we reckon all that is ſpent in abſolute *Sloth*, or doing of Nothing, with that which is ſpent in idle Employments or Amuſements, that amount to Nothing. *Sloth*, by bringing on Diſeaſes, abſolutely ſhortens Life. *Sloth, like Ruſt, conſumes faſter than Labour wears, while the uſed Key is always bright*, as *Poor Richard* ſays. But *Doſt thou love Life? then do not ſquander Time, for that's the Stuff Life is made of*, as *Poor Richard* ſays: How much more than is neceſſary do we ſpend in Sleep! forgetting that *The ſleeping Fox catches no Poultry*, and that *There will be ſleeping enough in the Grave*, as *Poor Richard* ſays. If Time be of all Things the moſt precious, *waſting Time* muſt be, as *Poor Richard* ſays, *The greateſt Prodigality*, ſince, as he elſewere tells us, *Loſt Time is never found again*; and what we call *Time enough, always proves little enough*. Let us then up and be doing, and doing to the Purpoſe; ſo by Diligence ſhall we do more with leſs Perplexity. *Sloth makes all Things difficult, but Induſtry all eaſy*, as *Poor Richard* ſays; and *He that riſeth late, muſt trot all Day, and ſhall ſcarce overtake his Buſineſs at Night*; while *Lazineſs travels ſo ſlowly, that Poverty ſoon overtakes him*, as we read in *Poor Richard*; who adds *Drive thy Buſineſs, let not that drive thee*; and *Early to Bed, and early to riſe, makes a Man healthy, wealthy and wiſe*.

It would be thought a hard Government that should tax its People one tenth Part of their *Time*, to be employed in its Service. But *Idleness* taxes many of us much more, if we reckon all that is spent in absolute *Sloth*, or doing of Nothing, with that which is spent in idle Employments or Amusements, that amount to nothing. *Sloth*, by bringing on Diseases, absolutely shortens Life. *Sloth, like Rust, consumes faster than Labor wears, while the used Key is always bright*, as *Poor Richard* says. But *Dost thou love Life? then do not squander Time, for that's the Stuff Life is made of*, as *Poor Richard* says: How much more than is necessary do we spend in Sleep! forgetting that *The sleeping Fox catches no Poultry*, and that *There will be sleeping enough in the Grave*, as *Poor Richard* says. If Time be of all Things the most precious, *wasting Time* must be, as *Poor Richard* says, *The greatest Prodigality*, since, as he elsewhere tells us, *Lost Time is never found again*, and what we call *Time enough, always proves little enough*. Let us then up and be doing, and doing to the Purpose; so by Diligence shall we do more with less Perplexity. *Sloth makes all Things difficult, but Industry all easy*, as *Poor Richard* says; and *He that riseth late, must trot all Day, and shall scarce overtake his Business at Night;* while *Laziness travels so slowly, that Poverty soon overtakes him*, as we read in *Poor Richard;* who adds, *Drive thy Business, let not that drive thee; and Early to Bed*, and *early to rise, makes a Man healthy, wealthy and wise.*

Father *Abraham*'s Speech.

So what fignifies *wifhing* and *hoping* for better Times. We may make thefe Times better if we beftir ourfelves. *Induftry need not wifh*, as *Poor Richard* fays, and *He that lives upon Hope will die fafting*. *There are no Gains without Pains* ; then *Help Hands, for I have no Lands*, or if I have, they are fmartly taxed. And, as *Poor Richard* likewife obferves, *He that hath a Trade hath an Eftate*, and *He that hath a Calling hath an Office of Profit and Honour* ; but then the *Trade* muft be worked at, and the *Calling* well followed, or neither the *Eftate*, nor the *Office*, will enable us to pay our Taxes. If we are induftrious we fhall never ftarve ; for, as *Poor Richard* fays, *At the working Man's Houfe* Hunger *looks in, but dares not enter*. Nor will the Bailiff or the Conftable enter, for *Induftry pays Debts, while Defpair encreafeth them*, fays *Poor Richard*. What though you have found no Treafure, nor has any rich Relation left you a Legacy, *Diligence is the Mother of Good-luck*, as *Poor Richard* fays, and *God gives all Things to Induftry* : Then *Plough deep, while Sluggards fleep, and you fhall have Corn to fell and to keep*, fays *Poor Dick*. Work while it is called To-day, for you know not how much you may be hindered To-morrow, which makes *Poor Richard* fay *One To-day is worth two To-morrows* ; and farther, *Have you fomewhat to do To-morrow ? do it To-day*. If you were a Servant, would you not be afhamed that a good Mafter fhould catch you idle ? Are you then your own Mafter ? *Be afhamed to catch*

So what signifies *wishing* and *hoping* for better Times. We may make these Times better if we bestir ourselves. *Industry need not wish*, as *Poor Richard* says, and *He that lives upon Hope will die fasting. There are no Gains, without Pains;* then *Help Hands for I have no Lands*, or if I have, they are smartly taxed. And, as *Poor Richard* likewise observes, *He that hath a Trade hath an Estate,* and *he that hath a Calling hath an Office of Profit and Honor;* but then the *Trade* must be worked at, and the *Calling* well followed, or neither the *Estate*, nor the *Office*, will enable us to pay our Taxes. If we are industrious we shall never starve; for, as *Poor Richard* says, *At the working Man's House* Hunger *looks in, but dares not enter.* Nor will the Bailiff or the Constable enter, for *Industry pays Debts, while Despair increaseth them*, says *Poor Richard.* What though you have found no Treasure, nor has any rich Relation left you a Legacy, *Diligence is the Mother of Good-luck*, as *Poor Richard* says, and *God gives all Things to Industry:* Then *Plough deep, while Sluggards sleep, and you shall have Corn to sell and to keep*, says *Poor Dick.* Work while it is called Today, for you know not how much you may be hindered Tomorrow, which makes *Poor Richard* say, *One Today is worth two Tomorrows*; and farther, *Have you somewhat to do Tomorrow? do it Today.* If you were a Servant, would you not be ashamed that a good Master should catch you idle? Are you then your own Master? *Be ashamed to catch*

9

yourself idle, as *Poor Dick* fays. When there is fo much to be done for your Self, your Family, your Country, and your gracious King, be up by Peep of Day : *Let not the Sun look down and fay*, IN-GLORIOUS HERE HE LIES. Handle your Tools without Mittens ;. remember that *The Cat in Gloves catches no Mice*, as *Poor Richard* fays. 'Tis true, there is much to be done, and perhaps you are weak-handed, but ftick to it fteadily, and you will fee great Effects, for *Conftant Dropping wears away Stones*, and *By Diligence and Patience the Moufe ate in two the Cable* ; and *Little Strokes fell great Oaks*, as *Poor Richard* fays in his Almanack, the Year I cannot juft now remember.

Methinks I hear fome of you fay, *Muft a Man afford himfelf no Leifure ?* I will tell thee, my Friends, what *Poor Richard* fays. *Employ thy Time well if thou meaneft to gain Leifure* ; and, *Since thou art not fure of a Minute, throw not away an Hour.* Leifure is Time for doing fomething ufeful ; this Leifure the diligent Man will obtain, but the lazy Man never ; fo that, as *Poor Richard* fays, *A Life of Leifure and a Life of Lazinefs are two Things.* Do you imagine that Sloth will afford you more Comfort than Labour ? No ; for, as *Poor Richard* fays, *Trouble fprings from Idlenefs, and grievous Toil from needlefs Eafe.* Many without Labour would live by their WITS only, but they break for want of Stock. Whereas Induftry gives Comfort, and Plenty, and Refpect. *Fly Pleafures and they'll follow you.* ---

yourself idle, as *Poor Dick* says. When there is so much to be done for Yourself, your Family, your Country, and your gracious King, be up by Peep of Day: *Let not the Sun look down and say*, INGLORIOUS HERE HE LIES. Handle your Tools without Mittens; remember that *The Cat in Gloves catches no Mice*, as *Poor Richard* says. 'Tis true, there is much to be done, and perhaps you are weakhanded, but stick to it steadily, and you will see great Effects, for *Constant Dropping wears away Stones*, and *By Diligence and Patience the Mouse ate in two the Cable*; and *Little Strokes fell great Oaks*, as *Poor Richard* says in his Almanack, the Year I cannot just now remember.

Methinks I hear some of you say, *Must a Man afford himself no Leisure?* I will tell thee, my Friends, what *Poor Richard* says. *Employ thy Time well if thou meanest to gain Leisure*; and, *Since thou art not sure of a Minute, throw not away an hour.* Leisure is Time for doing something useful; this Leisure the diligent Man will obtain, but the lazy Man never; so that, as *Poor Richard* says, *A Life of Leisure and a Life of Laziness are two Things.* Do you imagine that Sloth will afford you more Comfort than Labor? No; for, as *Poor Richard* says, *Trouble Springs from Idleness, and grievous Toil from needless Ease. Many without Labor would live by their* WITS *only, but they break for want of Stock.* Whereas Industry gives Comfort, and Plenty, and Respect. *Fly Pleasures, and they'll follow you.—*

Father *Abraham*'s Speech.

The diligent Spinner has a large Shift; and *Now I have a Sheep and a Cow, every Body bids me Good-Morrow*; all which is well faid by *Poor Richard*.

But with our Induftry, we muft likewife be *fteady fettled* and *careful*, and overfee our own Affairs *with our own Eyes*, and not truft too much to others; for, as *Poor Richard* fays.

> *I never faw an oft removed Tree,*
> *Nor yet an oft removed Family,*
> *That throve fo well as thofe that fettled be.*

And again, *Three-Removes is as bad as a Fire*; and again *Keep thy Shop, and thy Shop will keep thee*; and again, *If you would have your Bufinefs done, go; if not, fend.* And again,

> *He that by the Plough would thrive,*
> *Himfelf muft either hold or drive.*

And again, *The Eye of a Mafter will do more Work than both his Hands*; and again, *Want of Care does us more Damage than want of Knowledge*; and again, *Not to overfee Workmen is to leave them your Purfe open.* Trufting too much to others Care is the Ruin of many; for as the *Almanack* fays, *In the Affairs of this World, Men are faved, not by Faith, but by the Want of it*; but a Man's own Care is profitable; for, faith *Poor Dick, Learning is to the Studious*, and *Riches to the Careful*, as well as *Power to the Bold*, and *Heaven to the Virtuous*. And farther, *If you would have a faithful Servant, and one that you like,----ferve your Self.* And again, he advifeth to Circumfpection and

The diligent Spinner has a large Shift, and *Now I have a Sheep and a Cow, Everybody bids me Good Morrow;* all which is well said by *Poor Richard.*

But with our Industry, we must likewise be *Steady Settled* and *careful*, and oversee our own Affairs *with our own Eyes*, and not trust too much to others; for, as *Poor Richard* says,

> *I never Saw an oft removed Tree,*
> *Nor yet an oft removed Family,*
> *That throve so well as those that Settled be.*

And again, *Three removes is as bad as a Fire*; and again, *Keep the Shop, and thy Shop will keep thee*; and again, *If you would have your Business done; go; if not, send.* And again,

> *He that by the Plough would thrive,*
> *Himself must either hold or drive.*

And again, *The Eye of a Master will do more Work than both his Hands*; and again, *Want of Care does us more Damage than want of Knowledge*, and again, *Not to oversee Workmen is to leave them your Purse open.* Trusting too much to others Care is the Ruin of many; for, as the *Almanack* says, *In the Affairs of this World Men are Saved, not by Faith, but by the Want of it*; but a Man's own Care is profitable; for, faith *Poor Dick, Learning is to the Studious*, and *Riches to the Careful*, as well as *Power to the Bold*, and *Heaven to the Virtuous.* And farther, *If you would have a faithful Servant*, and one that you like,—serve yourself. And again, he adviseth to Circumspection and

Father *Abraham*'s Speech.

Care, even in the smallest Matters, because sometimes *A little Neglect may breed great Mischief* ; adding, *For want of a Nail the Shoe was lost* ; *for want of a Shoe the Horse was lost* ; *and for want of a Horse the Rider was lost*, being overtaken and slain by the Enemy, all for want of Care about a Horse-shoe Nail.

So much for Industry, my Friends, and Attention to one's own Business ; but to these we must add *Frugality*, if we would make our *Industry* more certainly successful. A Man may, if he knows not how to save as he gets, *keep his Nose all his Life to the Grindstone*, and die not worth a *Groat* at last. *A fat Kitchen makes a lean Will*, as *Poor Richard* says ; and,

Many Estates are spent in the Getting,
Since Women for Tea forsook Spinning and Knitting,
And Men for Punch forsook Hewing and Splitting.

If you would be wealthy, says he in another Almanack, *think of Saving, as well as of Getting :* *The* Indies *have not made* Spain *rich because her* Outgoes *are greater than her* Incomes. Away then with your expensive Follies, and you will not have so much Cause to complain of hard Times, heavy Taxes, and chargeable Famlies ; for, as *Poor Dick* says,

Women and Wine, Game and Deceit,
Make the Wealth small, and the Wants great.
And farther, *What maintains one Vice, would bring up two Children.* You may think, perhaps, that a

Care, even in the smallest Matters, because sometimes *A little Neglect may breed great Mischief;* adding, *For want of a Nail the Shoe was lost; for want of a Shoe the Horse was lost; and for want of a Horse the Rider was lost,* being overtaken and slain by the Enemy, all for want of Care about a Horseshoe Nail.

So much for Industry, my Friends, and Attention to one's own Business; but to these we must add *Frugality,* if we would make our Industry more certainly successful. A Man may, if he knows not how to save as he gets, *keep his Nose all his Life to the Grindstone,* and die not worth a *Groat* at last. *A fat Kitchen makes a lean Will,* as *Poor Richard* says; and,

Many Estates are Spent in the Getting,
Since Women for Tea forsook Spinning and Knitting, And Men for Punch forsook Hewing and Splitting.

If you would be wealthy, says he, in another Almanack, *think of Saving as well as of Getting. The* Indies *have not made* Spain *rich because her* Outgoes *are greater than her* Incomes. Away then with your expensive Follies, and you will not have so much Cause to complain of hard Times, heavy Taxes, and chargeable Families; for, as *Poor Dick* says,

Women and Wine, Game and Deceit,

Make the Wealth small, and the Wants great. And farther, *What maintains one Vice, would bring up two Children.* You may think, perhaps, that a *little* Tea, or a *little* Punch now and then, Diet a *little* more coſtly, Clothes a *little* finer, and a *little* Entertainment, now and then, can be no *great* Matter; but remember what *Poor Richard* ſays, *Many a Little makes a Mickle* ; and farther, *Beware of* little *Expences. A ſmall Leak will ſink a great Ship.* And again, *Who Dainties love, ſhall Beggars prove.* And moreover, *Fools make Feaſts and wiſe Men eat them.*

Here you are all got together at this Vendue of *Fineries* and *Knicknacks.* You call them *Goods,* but if you do not take Care, they will prove *Evils* to ſome of you. You expect they will be ſold *cheap,* and perhaps they may for leſs than they cóſt ; but if you have no Occaſion for them, they muſt be *dear* to you. Remember what *Poor Richard* ſays, *Buy what thou haſt no Need of, and ere long thou ſhalt ſell thy Neceſſaries.* And again, *At a great Pennyworth Pauſe a While.* : He means, that perhaps the Cheapneſs is *apparent* only, and not *real* ; or the Bargain, by ſtraitning thee in thy Buſineſs, may do thee more Harm than Good. For in another Place he ſays *Many have been ruined by buying good Pennyworths.* Again *Poor Richard* ſays, *'Tis fooliſh to lay out Money in a Purchaſe of Repentance ;* and yet this Folly is practiſed every Day at Vendues, for want of minding the Almanack. *Wiſe Men,* as *Poor Dick* ſays, *learn by others Harms, Fools ſcarcely by their own* ; but *Felix quem faciunt aliena Pericula cautum.* Many a One, for the Sake of Finery on the Back, have gone

little Tea, or a *little* Punch now and then, Diet a *little* more costly, Clothes a *little* finer, and a *little* Entertainment, now and then, can be no *great* Matter; but remember what *Poor Richard* says, *Many* a Little *makes a Mickle*; and farther, *Beware of little Expenses. A small Leak will sink a great Ship.* And again, *Who Dainties love, shall Beggars Prove.* And moreover, *Fools make Feasts, and wise Men eat them.*

Here you are all got together at this vendue of *Fineries* and *Knickknacks.* You call them *Goods,* but if you do not take Care, they will prove *Evils* to some of you. You expect they will be sold *cheap,* and perhaps they may for less than they cost; but if you have no Occasion for them, they must be *dear* to you. Remember what *Poor Richard* says, *Buy what thou hast no Need of, and ere long thou shalt sell thy Necessaries.* And again, *At a great Pennyworth Pause a While*: He means, that perhaps the Cheapness is *apparent* only, and not *real*; or the Bargain, by straitening thee in thy Business, may do thee more Harm than Good. For in another Place he says *Many have been ruined by buying good Pennyworths.* Again, *Poor Richard* says, *'Tis foolish to lay out Money in a Purchase of Repentance*; and yet this Folly is practiced every Day at Vendues, for want of minding the Almanack. *Wise Men*, as *Poor Dick* says, *learn by others' Harms, Fools scarcely by their own*; but *Felix quem faciunt aliena pericula cautum.* Many a One, for the Sake of Finery on the Back, have gone

17

with a hungry Belly, and half ftarved their Families. *Silks and Sattins, Scarlet and Velvets* (as *Poor Richard* fays) *put out the Kitchen Fire.* Thefe are not the *Neceffaries* of Life, they can fcarcely be called the *Conveniencies* ; and yet only becaufe they look pretty, how many *want* to *have* them. The *artificial* Wants of Mankind thus become more numerous than the *natural* ; and, as *Poor Dick* fays, *For one* poor *Perfon, there are an hundred* indigent. By thefe, and other Extravagancies, the Genteel are reduced to Poverty, and forced to borrow of thofe whom they formerly defpifed, but who, through *Induftry* and *Frugality*, have maintained their Standing ; in which Cafe it appears plainly, that *A Ploughman on his Legs is higher than a Gentleman on his Knees,* as *Poor Richard* fays. Perhaps they have had a fmall Eftate left them, which they knew not the Getting of ; they think *'tis Day and will never be Night* ; that a little to be fpent out of *fo much*, is not worth minding ; (*A Child and a Fool,* as *Poor Richard* fays, *imagine* Twenty Shillings *and Twenty Years can never be fpent*) but, *Always taking out of the Meal-Tub and never putting in foon comes to the Bottom* ; then, as *Poor Dick* fays, *When the Well's dry they know the Worth of Water.* But this they might have known before, if they had taken his Advice. *If you would know the Value of Money, go and try to borrow fome* ; for, *He that goes a borrow-*

with a hungry Belly, and half starved their Families; *Silks and Satins, Scarlet and Velvets* (as *Poor Richard* says) *put out the Kitchen Fire*. These are not the *Necessaries* of Life, they can scarcely be called the *Conveniencies*; and yet only because they look pretty, how many *want* to *have* them. The *artificial* Wants of Mankind thus become more numerous than the *natural*; and, as *Poor Dick* says, *For one poor Person, there are an hundred* indigent. By these, and other Extravagancies, the Genteel are reduced to Poverty, and forced to borrow of those whom they formerly despised, but who, through *Industry* and *Frugality*, have maintained their Standing; in which Case it appears plainly, that *A Ploughman on his Legs is higher than a Gentleman on his Knees*, as *Poor Richard* says. Perhaps they have had a small Estate left them, which they knew not the Getting of; they think *'tis Day and will never be Night*; that a little to be spent out of *so much*, is not worth minding; (*A Child and a Fool*, as *Poor Richard* says, *imagine* Twenty Shillings *and Twenty Years can never be spent*) but, *Always taking out of the Meal-Tub, and never putting in soon comes to the Bottom*; then, as *Poor Dick* says, *When the Well's dry they know the Worth of Water*. But this they might have known before, if they had taken his Advice. *If you would know the Value of Money, go and try to borrow some*; for, *He that goes a borrow-*

Father *Abraham*'s Speech.

ing goes a sorrowing ; and indeed so does he that lends to such People, when he goes *to get it in again.----Poor Dick* farther advises and says,

Fond Pride of Dress, *is sure a very Curse.*

E'er Fancy *yon consult, consult your Purse.*

And again, *Pride is as loud a Beggar as Want, and a great deal more saucy.* When you have bought one fine Thing you must buy ten more, that your Appearance may be all of a Piece ; but Poor *Dick* says, *'Tis easier to* supprefs *the first Desire, than to* satisfy *all that follow it.* And 'tis as truly Folly for the Poor to *ape* the Rich, as for the Frog to swell in order to equal the Ox,

Great Estates may venture more,

But little Boats should keep near Shore.

'Tis however a Folly soon punished ; for *Pride that dines on Vanity sups on Contempt,* as Poor *Richard* says. And, in another Place, *Pride breakfasted with Plenty, dined with Poverty, and supped with Infamy.* And, after all, of what Use is this *Pride of Appearance,* for which so much is risqued, so much is suffered ? It cannot promote Health, or ease Pain ; it makes no Increase of Merit in the Person ; it creates Envy, it hastens Misfortune.

What is a Butterfly? At best

He's but a Catterpillar drest.

The gaudy Fop's his Picture just ;

as Poor *Richard* says.

But what Madness must it be to *run in Debt* for these Superfluities ! We are offered, by the Terms

20

ing goes a sorrowing; and indeed so does he that lends to such people, when he goes *to get it in again.—Poor Dick* farther advises, and says,

> *Fond* Pride if Dress, *is sure a very Curse.*
> *E'er* Fancy *you consult, consult your Purse.*

And again, *Pride is as loud a Beggar as Want, and a great deal more saucy.* When you have bought one fine Thing you must buy ten more, that your Appearance maybe all of a Piece; but Poor *Dick* says, *'Tis easier to* suppress *the first desire, than to* satisfy *all that follow it.* And 'tis as truly Folly for the Poor to *ape* the Rich, as for the Frog to swell, in order to equal the Ox.

> *Great Estates may venture more,*
> *But little Boats should keep near Shore.*

'Tis however a Folly soon punished; for *Pride that dines on Vanity sups on Contempt,* as Poor *Richard* says. And in another Place, *Pride breakfasted with Plenty, dined with Poverty, and supped with Infamy.* And, after all, of what Use is this *Pride of Appearance,* for which so much is risked, so much is suffered? It cannot promote Health; or ease Pain; it makes no Increase of Merit in the Person; it creates Envy, it hastens Misfortune.

> *What is a Butterfly? At best*
> *He's but a Caterpillar dressed.*
> *The gaudy Fop's his Picture just,*

as Poor Richard says.

But what Madness must it be to *run in Debt* for these Superfluities! We are offered, by the Terms

21

of this Vendue, *Six Months Credit* ; and that, perhaps, has induced some of us to attend it, because
we cannot spare the ready Money, and hope now
to be fine without it. But, ah ! think what you
do when you run in Debt : *You give to another
Power over your Liberty.* If you cannot pay at
the Time, you will be ashamed to see your Creditor ; you will be in Fear when you speak to him ;
you will make poor, pitiful, sneaking Excuses,
and by Degrees come to lose your Veracity, and
sink into base downright Lying ; for, as Poor
Richard says, *The second Vice is Lying, the first is
running in Debt.* And again, to the same Purpose,
Lying rides upon Debt's Back. Whereas a freeborn *Englishman* ought not to be ashamed or afraid
to see or speak to any Man living. But Poverty
often deprives a Man of all Spirit and Virtue.
'Tis hard for an empty Bag to stand upright, as *Poor
Richard* truly says. What would you think of
that Prince, or that Government, who should issue
an Edict forbiding you to dress like a Gentleman
or a Gentlewoman, on Pain of Imprisonment or
Servitude ? Would you not say that you are free,
have a Right to dress as you please, and that such
an Edict would be a Breach of your Privileges,
and such a Government tyrannical ? And yet you
are about to put yourself under that Tyranny, when
you run in Debt for such Dress ! Your Creditor
has Authority, at his Pleasure, to deprive you of
your Liberty, by confining you in Goal for Life,

of this Vendue, *Six Months Credit*; and that, perhaps, has induced some of us to attend it, because we cannot spare the ready Money, and hope now to be fine without it. But, ah! think what you do when you run in Debt: *You give to another Power over your liberty.* If you cannot pay at the Time, you will be ashamed to see your Creditor; you will be in Fear when you speak to him; you will make poor, pitiful, sneaking Excuses, and by Degrees come to lose your Veracity, and sink into base downright Lying; for, as Poor *Richard* says, *The Second Vice is Lying, the first is running in Debt.* And again, to the same Purpose, *Lying rides upon Debt's back.* Whereas a freeborn *Englishman* ought not to be ashamed or afraid to see or speak to any Man living. But Poverty often deprives a Man of all Spirit and Virtue. *'Tis hard for an empty Bag to stand upright,* as *Poor Richard* truly says. What would you think of that Prince, or that Government, who should issue an Edict forbidding you to dress like a Gentleman or Gentlewoman, on Pain of Imprisonment or Servitude? Would you not say that you are free, have a Right to dress as you please, and that such an Edict would be a Breach of your Privileges, and such a Government tyrannical? And yet you are about to put yourself under that Tyranny when you run in Debt for such Dress! Your Creditor has Authority, at his Pleasure, to deprive you of your Liberty, by confining you in Jail for Life,

or to fell you for a Servant, if you fhould not be
able to pay him! When you have got your Bargain, you may, perhaps, think little of Payment;
but *Creditors* (Poor *Richard* tells us) *have better
Memories than Debtors*; and in another Place fays,
*Creditors are a fuperftitious Sect, great Obfervers of
fet Days and Times.* The Day comes round before
you are aware, and the Demand is made before you
are prepared to fatisfy it. Or if you bear your
Debt in Mind, the Term which at firft feemed fo
long, will, as it leffens, appear extremely fhort.
Time will feem to have added Wings to his Heels as
well as Shoulders. *Thofe have a fhort Lent* (faith
Poor Richard) *who owe Money to be paid at Eafter.*
Then fince, as he fays, *The Borrower is a Slave to
the Lender, and the Debtor to the Creditor*, difdain
the Chain, preferve your Freedom, and maintain
your Independency. Be *induftrious* and *free*; be
frugal and *free*. At prefent perhaps you may think
yourfelf in thriving Circumftances, and that you
can bear a little Extravagance without Injury; but
  For Age and Want fave while you may.
  No Morning-Sun lafts a whole Day;
as *Poor Richard* fays.---Gain may be temporary and
uncertain, but ever while you live, Expence is conftant and certain; and *'Tis eafier to build two
Chimnies, than to keep one in Fuel*, as *Poor Richard*
fays. So *rather go to Bed fupperlefs than rife in Debt.*
  Get what you can, and what you get hold;
  'Tis the Stone that will turn all your Lead into Gold.
as Poor *Richard* fays.

or to sell you for a Servant, if you should not be able to pay him! When you have got your Bargain, you may, perhaps, think little of Payment; but *Creditors* (Poor *Richard* tells us) *have better Memories than Debtors*; and in another Place says, *Creditors are a superstitious Sect, great Observers of set Days and Times.* The Day comes round before you are aware, and the Demand is made before you are prepared to satisfy it. Or if you bear your Debt in Mind, the Term which at first seemed so long, will, as it lessens, appear extremely short. *Time* will seem to have added Wings to his Heels as well as Shoulders. *Those have a short Lent* (saith *Poor Richard*) *who owe Money to be paid at Easter.* Then since, as he says, *The Borrower is a Slave to the Lender, and the Debtor to the Creditor*, disdain the Chain, preserve your Freedom; and maintain your Independency. Be *industrious* and *free*; be *frugal* and *free*. At present perhaps you may think yourself in thriving Circumstances, and that you can bear a little Extravagance without Injury; but,

> *For Age and Want, save while you may;*
> *No Morning-Sun lasts a whole Day;*

as *Poor Richard* says.—Gain may be temporary and uncertain, but ever while you live, Expense is constant and certain; and *'Tis easier to build two Chimneys, than to keep one in Fuel*, as *Poor Richard* says. So *rather go to Bed supperless than rise in Debt.*

> *Get what you can, and what you get hold;*
> *'Tis the Stone that will turn all your Lead into Gold*, as Poor *Richard* says.

Father *Abraham*'s Speech.

And when you have got the Philofopher's Stone, fure you will no longer complain of bad Times, or the Difficulty of paying Taxes.

This Doctrine, my Friends, is *Reafon* and *Wifdom*; but, after all, do not depend too much upon your own *Induftry*, and *Frugality*, and *Prudence*, though excellent Things, for they may all be blafted without the Blefling of Heaven; and therefore afk that Blefling humbly, and be not uncharitable to thofe that at prefent feem to want it, but comfort and help them. Remember *Job* fuffered, and was afterwards profperous.

And now to conclude. *Experience keeps a dear School, but Fools will learn in no other, and fcarce in that*; for it is true, *We may give Advice, but we cannot give Conduct*, as *Poor Richard* fays: However, remember this, *They that won't be counfelled, can't be helped*, as *Poor Richard* fays: And farther, that *If you will not hear Reafon fhe'll furely rap your Knuckles.*"

Thus the old Gentleman ended his Harangue. The People heard it, and approved the Doctrine, and immediately practifed the Contrary, juft as if it had been a common Sermon; for the Vendue opened, and they began to buy extravagantly, notwithftanding all his Cautions, and their own Fear of Taxes.----I found the good Man had thoroughly ftudied my Almanacks, and digefted all I had dropt on thofe Topicks during the Courfe of five-and-

And when you have got the Philosopher's Stone, sure you will no longer complain of bad Times, or the Difficulty of paying Taxes.

This Doctrine, my Friends, is *Reason* and *Wisdom*; but, after all, do not depend too much upon your own *Industry*, and *Frugality*, and *Prudence*, though excellent Things, for they may all be blasted without the Blessing of Heaven; and therefore ask that Blessing humbly, and be not uncharitable to those that at present seem to want it, but comfort and help them. Remember *Job* suffered, and was afterwards prosperous.

And now to conclude. *Experience keeps a dear School, but Fools will learn in no other, and scarce in that*; for it is true, *We may give Advice, but we cannot give Conduct*, as *Poor Richard* says: However, remember this, *They that won't be counseled, can't be helped*, as *Poor Richard* says: And farther, that *If you will not hear Reason, she'll surely rap your Knuckles.*"

Thus the old Gentleman ended his Harangue. The People heard it, and approved the Doctrine, and immediately practiced the Contrary, just as if it had been a common Sermon; for the Vendue opened, and they began to buy extravagantly, notwithstanding all his Cautions, and their own Fear of Taxes.—I found the good Man had thoroughly studied my Almanacks, and digested all I had dropped on those Topics during the Course of five-and-twenty Years. The frequent Mention he made of me, muft have tired any one elfe, but my Vanity was wonderfully delighted with it, though I was confcious that not a tenth Part of the Wifdom was my own which he afcribed to me, but rather the *Gleanings* I had made of the Senfe of all Ages and Nations. However, I refolved to be the better for the Echo of it ; and thô I had at firft determined to buy Stuff for a new Coat, I went away refolved to wear my old One a little longer. *Reader*, if thou wilt do the fame, thy Profit will be as great as mine.

I am, as ever,

Thine to ferve thee,

Richard Saunders.

July 7. 1757

twenty Years. The frequent Mention he made of me, must have tired any one else, but my Vanity was wonderfully delighted with it, though I was conscious that not a tenth Part of the Wisdom was my own which he ascribed to me, but rather the *Gleanings* I had made of the Sense of all Ages and Nations. However, I resolved to be the better for the Echo of it; and though I had at first determined to buy Stuff for a new Coat, I went away resolved to wear my old One a little longer. *Reader*, if thou wilt do the same, thy Profit will be as great as mine.

I am, as ever,

Thine to serve thee,

Richard Saunders

July 7, 1757